Lawson-Westen House

The biggest
danger,
that of losing
oneself,
can pass
off in
the world
as quietly
as if
it were
nothing;
every other
loss,
an arm,
a leg,
five dollars,
a wife, etc
is bound
to be
noticed.

Kierkegaard

To Damon
Hey you, would you help me to carry the stone?

Pink Floyd

To Jessica
Hey you, don't help them to bury the light.

Pink Floyd

Eric Owen Moss

Phaidon Press Limited
Regent's Wharf
All Saints Street
London N1 9PA

First published 1995

© 1995 Phaidon Press Limited

ISBN 0 7148 3259 6

A CIP catalogue record for
this book is available from
the British Library.

Printed in Singapore

Lawson-Westen House
Eric Owen Moss

James Steele
ARCHITECTURE IN DETAIL

Φ

Eric Owen Moss has designed relatively few residences, not because of a lack of opportunity; rather because of a lack of time. As a result of his historic association with the enlightened developer Frederick Norton Smith, who has carved out a large portion of Culver City – an area located south of the Santa Monica Freeway – as his field of endeavour, Moss has been preoccupied with large-scale commercial buildings which are gradually conglomerating to create a small city in this community to the west of Los Angeles that was once famed as the location of the major film studios in the twenties. In the Ince, 8522 National Boulevard, Samitaur and Hayden Tract Complexes, as well as in S.P.A.R.C I T Y, to be built in the air rights zone over the railroad running through the area, Eric Owen Moss has been able to explore what he has termed 'emotive geometries' and the way these can apply to a new level of urban consciousness.

1

2

1 Greene and Greene, Gamble House, Pasadena, 1908. The house helped to establish a precedent for indoor/outdoor living space in Southern California residential architecture.
2 Frank Lloyd Wright extended the precedent of the Gamble House by incorporating a central courtyard into his design of the Barnsdall House, Los Angeles, 1921.
3 Frank Gehry, Schnabel House, Brentwood, California, 1990. The house comments on many aspects of the urban character of Los Angeles.

4 Eric Owen Moss, Petal House, West Los Angeles', 1982.
5 Rudolf Schindler, King's Road House, Los Angeles, 1921, ingeniously wraps around two separate courtyards which are used as outdoor rooms.
6 Eric Owen Moss, Lawson-Westen House, Brentwood, California, 1993.

3

While these projects have allowed him to examine issues related to internalized environments which permit many people to work together in carefully determined surroundings, the final users were unknown to him, and might also change depending on market forces. Both the scale and function of these complexes, as well as the inherent anonymity of those they are intended for, have prevented him from using them as the means for a deeper reading of the contemporary condition which, in Los Angeles, has typically been achieved through the design of a house. Earlier examples of Los Angeles/Southern California residences such as the Gamble House by Greene and Greene, the Barnsdall House by Frank Lloyd Wright, King's Road House by Rudolf Schindler, the Case Study series houses, as well as the more recent Schnabel Houses by Frank Gehry, all demonstrate the important role that residential architecture has typically played as an accurate barometer of social change in the region.

5

4

Moss' highly publicized Petal House in West Los Angeles, 1982, was instrumental in subverting the traditional concept of what a home, especially as designed by an architect, should look like. Its context, in the midst of a typical suburban neighbourhood, provided Moss with a particularly fertile resource; he responded by using the materials and forms around the site to provoke debate about the architect's abdication of responsibility for popular housing, among other things.[1] The Lawson-Westen commission, which followed six years later, however, offered him the chance to expand that debate much further into a different stratum of social commentary. Intended for a 70x180ft (21.3x54.8m) flat site at Westgate Avenue, between Sunset and San Vincente on the north and south and Barrington and Bundy on the east and west, the house was to be located in one of the wealthier neighbourhoods in Los Angeles' 'West Side'. It was surrounded by high hedges on all sides with the possibility of a view to the Pacific.

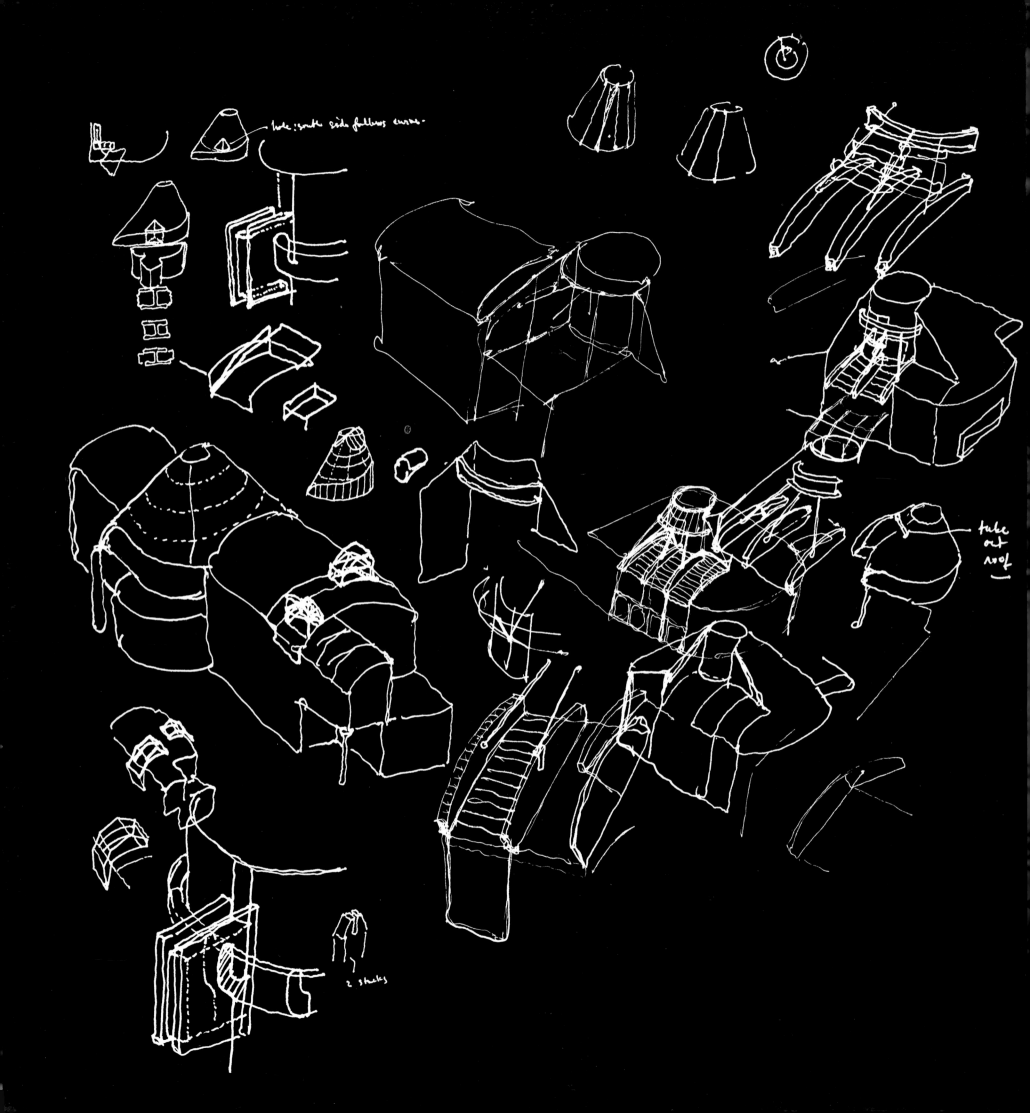

From client letter to brief The axiom that there can be no great architecture without an informed and enlightened client has been strengthened once again by this example, since both individuals for whom the house was designed took an active role in its realization. Extensive correspondence between the clients and Moss essentially became the architect's brief, the letters being annotated in minute detail before being transcribed into a list of functional requirements. The essence of the house, as it finally came to be, can be seen to emerge from the architect's notations and sketches in the margins of those letters, the unknown territory of the design idea tentatively circumscribed by both parties through written communication. In the earliest stream-of-consciousness 'wish list' that the clients provided, which begins with reference to elements in past houses that they wanted to replicate, there is a consistent emphasis on height and space, of 'room to breathe'; in fact this phrase is repeated so fre-

7 Moss' conceptual sketches capture the spirit of the clients' brief.
8, 9 Aerial views of the Lawson-Westen House show the typical size of rectilinear residential lots in the neighbourhood, which prompted the clients to request an atrium design.
10 Philip Johnson, Glass House, New Canaan, Connecticut, 1951. The house was put forward as an example of the degree of openness the clients wanted, in part, of their new home.

quently that the architect notes them in numerical order. The clients' first list culminates in a request for engaging detail and an admitted attraction towards 'living rooms with high ceilings, crossed beams, skylights', and 'something up there, a construction that makes one look up, like a cathedral'. Without further elaboration, the notion of a dominant, soaring space became a tacit prerequisite, the most defined space in the scheme. Related to that wish was an expressed desire for a consolidation of rooms rather than a series of small ones; specifically, 'a living room that's spacious, truly lived in (and not a formal appendage), comfortable, appropriate for looking at art and listening to music, perhaps incorporating the dining area as well as the kitchen, seductive for parties and entertaining, even large gatherings'.[2] In the margin, along with his sketches and other notes, the architect reiterated the word 'seductive', and encircled it boldly.

After reinforcing this second idea of a large and informal living area with a high ceiling that is combined with the dining room and kitchen, the clients then shifted their attention to the relationship they wanted to establish between the interior and exterior, citing desirable precedents from their own experience and reading including, most notably, the Glass House by Philip Johnson in New Canaan, Connecticut – a house which gains privacy only by its location in the middle of an immense, heavily wooded area. The curiously dichotomous condition that the Glass House represents, one of privacy through openness and the exaggeration of the principle of a free-flow of space which was formally adopted as part of the unwritten credo of the Modern Movement, could not easily be recreated on a much smaller, rectangular lot on the west side of Los Angeles.

The clients therefore decided to express an adaptive stratagem. Calling their own adaptation 'a garden home in the middle of a city', they described a mental image of a circular house, with outer and inner walls made entirely of glass, surrounded by a rectilinear solid 'container' wall for privacy from the neighbours, with a garden in between. 'In the circle inside the home,' the clients continued, 'was another garden, and as a result, from anywhere in the house … one could see two gardens: an outer and an inner one.'[13] Marking his clients' request with the notation 'double view' in the margin of the letter, Moss also sketched a circular form in the middle of a larger series of orthogonal containers, connected by diagonal spokes labelled 'art walls'. At this point, in his initial reaction to this letter of 11 November 1988, Moss had established the basic elements of the *parti*.

As finally translated into plan, these ideas and the architect's initial *parti* resulted in an elongated rectangle congruent with the northern site boundary, favouring Westgate Avenue

8

11

13

14

11, 13, 14 The large central core of the house is contained by several steel rings, here shown before they were incorporated into the walls.
12 A concrete portal frame comprises most of the wall facing the main entrance.
15 The front door, casually wrapped around a corner, is characteristic of the architect's whimsical approach to building elements that are normally taken for granted.

12

on the east. This allowed for as much green space as possible on the rest of the lot, with an intersecting circle placed southwest of centre. As the fulcrum of the entire scheme, the 30ft (9.14m) diameter circle which contains the kitchen, is the literal continuation of the mental image of a house conveyed to the architect by his clients, the 'art walls' spinning out from becoming the remainder of the functions required. In a technique used to equal effect both by Frank Lloyd Wright and Charles Rennie Mackintosh, Moss has intentionally located the main entrances, for both the owners and their visitors, at the end of the rectangle rather than at a perpendicular axis with it, so that the spaces leading up to the major conical volume may be experienced sequentially, thus providing gradually enlarged, anticipatory views through the entire length of the house rather than an abrupt confrontation as both a first and final act.

15

Paradox begins at the front door Unlike the more conventional entrance provided for the clients, which follows on from a two-car garage opening onto Westgate, the front doors for visitors continue a paradoxical dialogue that runs throughout Moss' preceding work and especially his conversions at 8522 National Boulevard, where the historical expectation of each door is re-examined in various permutations. Deliberately placed at a right angle to each other, the doors are an introduction to what Moss has described as a 'hedonism of assembly' indulged throughout the house. As he says: 'There is a split in the house between limited and limitless, known and unknown. I tried very hard to build that into the experience of the building … You could consider the front door as experimental in a small way; its combining pieces of wood door and glass door gives you aspects of *both*; it gives you something else. The door is not a Venturi joke; it raises the possibility that things can be understood in a different way.'[14]

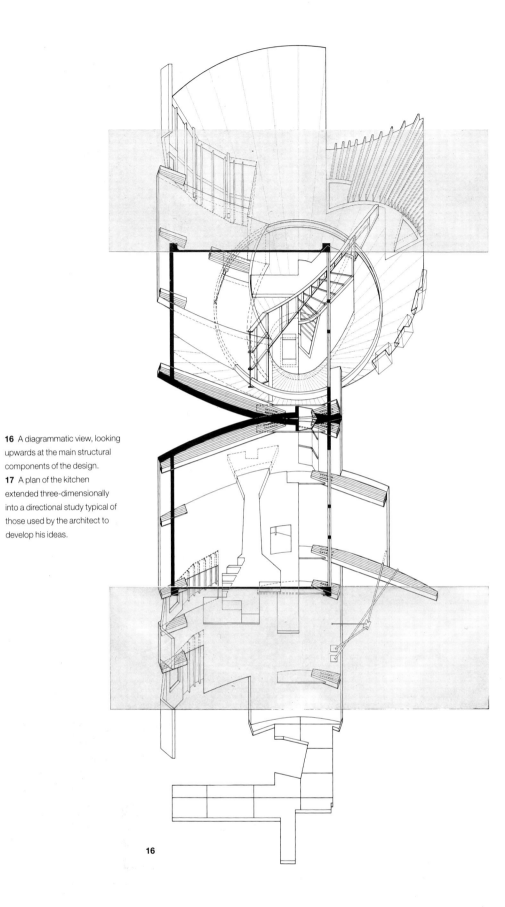

16 A diagrammatic view, looking upwards at the main structural components of the design.
17 A plan of the kitchen extended three-dimensionally into a directional study typical of those used by the architect to develop his ideas.

16

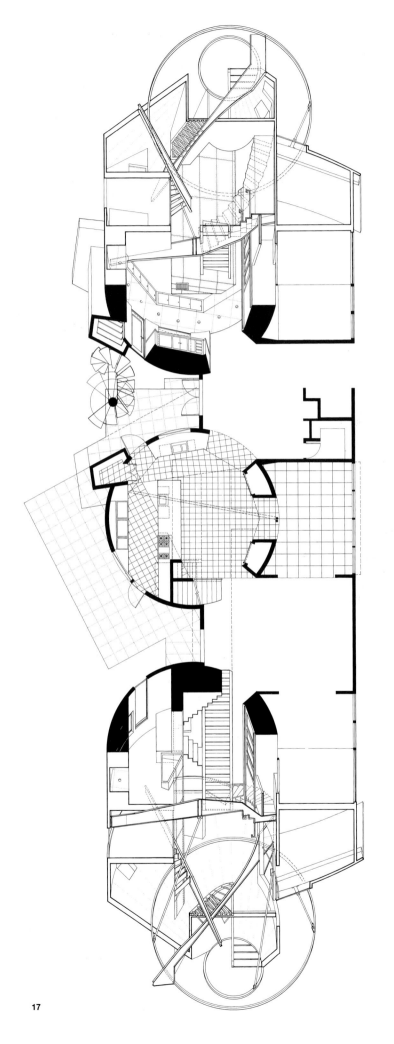

17

The 'aspects of both' Moss refers to is also a deftly abstract rendition of the client's first wish for a glass wall, quickly tempered by the solidity required in western Los Angeles, expanded as a theme throughout the house. A second, more graphic instance of this solidity is a steel fireplace, soaring for a full two storeys up the living room wall nearest the door, which provides an unexpected sculptural object serving as an intermediary between a relatively low entrance foyer and the rapid increase in vertical scale beyond. The fireplace also befits the genre of 'a hedonism of assembly', while innovative metalwork, crafted to the architect's specifications by Tom Farrage, is another consistent theme in Moss' own work. First announced on Westgate by the wide, galvanized sheet-metal gate that separates the walkway to the house from the street, this theme is reinforced by a truss-like strut that diagonally braces the single completion of the amputated glu-lam beams supporting the vaulted living room roof, and the cement-plaster wall

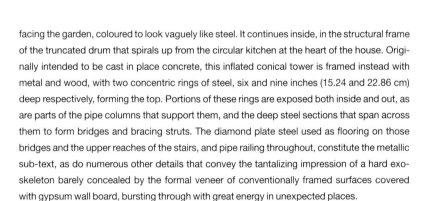

19

20

facing the garden, coloured to look vaguely like steel. It continues inside, in the structural frame of the truncated drum that spirals up from the circular kitchen at the heart of the house. Originally intended to be cast in place concrete, this inflated conical tower is framed instead with metal and wood, with two concentric rings of steel, six and nine inches (15.24 and 22.86 cm) deep respectively, forming the top. Portions of these rings are exposed both inside and out, as are parts of the pipe columns that support them, and the deep steel sections that span across them to form bridges and bracing struts. The diamond plate steel used as flooring on those bridges and the upper reaches of the stairs, and pipe railing throughout, constitute the metallic sub-text, as do numerous other details that convey the tantalizing impression of a hard exoskeleton barely concealed by the formal veneer of conventionally framed surfaces covered with gypsum wall board, bursting through with great energy in unexpected places.

18 The soaring stair marks the transition from living room to kitchen.
19 The sculptural steel fireplace is encountered soon after entering the front door.
20 A view towards the living room from the circular kitchen.
21 The dining area is adjacent to the kitchen, and is sufficiently enclosed to provide privacy.

The kitchen, which can be seen soon after entering the living room from the foyer, is undoubtedly the vortex of that energy, generating the major spaces of the house on both the ground and first floor, in plan, and satisfying the clients' original wish for openness, expressed as 'a sense of visual space … not just into an enclosed work space'.[5] While it does that, with a wide opening to the dining room, living room, playroom and garden, to allow for communication and observation between each of these while food is being prepared, there is also a deep service zone around the perimeter of the circle through which these openings penetrate, which includes the main stair leading to the upper levels. On the first floor, this service zone which faces inwards, as counter area and storage space in the kitchen, flips outwards here, becoming fireplaces and deepened doorways as an extroverted equivalent of the service buffer below. As Moss describes the importance of the circle as the generator of spatial form:

21

The kitchen is where [the owners] entertain, so that space became the focal element of the building – the place to hang out. A cone becomes the roof shape of the cylindrical kitchen, but the center of the cone is not the center of the cylinder. The cone top is cut off and you get the ocean view deck. The cone is sliced vertically, and that cut gives you a curve, which is parabolic. Pull the curve toward the street and you have the vaulted roof. That's the idealized vault. The only literal instance is one rib fully extended at the entrance.

There's a mapping of the kitchen in plan, that sets a series of points and suggests plan options, or rules. But as those rules are interpreted in the section, the connection between the hypothetical logic of the plan and the reality of the section seem to diminish. The sectional consequences don't give back the plan.

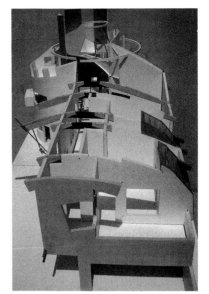

22

22 Countless study models helped the architect evolve the complex geometries of the house.
23 Much of the kitchen area is occupied by a counter area and storage space, with the winding stair visible from below.
24 A study model of the central core without its covering roof shows the configuration of the structure.
25 The steel bands that support the core are only now visible in segments of the space.

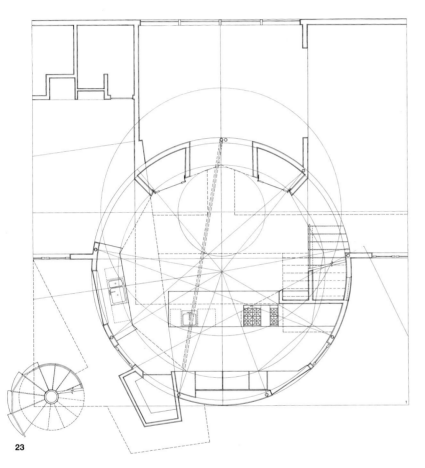

23

The geometric order of the cone/cylinder kitchen depends first on the center of a square, which is the geographic center of the site. The apex of the vaulted roof is drawn through that center point. A ring beam concentric to this center supports the cone roof. The kitchen cylinder is adjusted to the south, tangent to one edge of the square. Cone and cylinder amend one another, creating a volume which is both.[6]

Far from being an abstract influence on the character of the space, the formative geometric order that originates from it is completely legible, above the pragmatic concerns inherent in kitchen design. As a result of advice from many different sources, including professional kitchen consultants, the final layout of the custom-built counters, concentrated along the southern wall of the drum and facing the garden, is extremely functional – a gourmet cook's

25

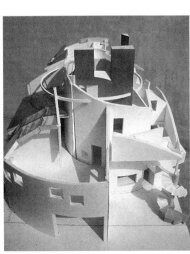

24

dream. In spite of the space available, work areas are organized into an efficient, linear galley, with a separate area for pastry off to one side. A trapezoidal pantry, considered important enough to be the only volume to disrupt the smoothly curving wall of the drum, indicates the status accorded to storage. The pantry shelves are intended for food, while all the awkwardly shaped equipment needed for preparation, normally so difficult to place, is located elsewhere, near the stove top and oven. Large hinged wooded racks, which retract into the wall, make selection easy and also transform the cooking equipment which is normally hidden behind cabinet doors into artful objects on display when the rack is open. This glorification of utilitarian elements is carried over into the surfaces, where fine wood and polished marble replace the synthetic composites typical of many kitchens; allowing for a sophisticated elevation of routine associations, as well as their realignment, which can be found throughout the house.

The stair leading to the first floor, just visible from the living room, with two projecting risers and treads acting to delineate further that space from the kitchen, has one straight and one curving side, as does Moss' subsequent design for 'The Box' adjacent to 8522 National Boulevard, which shares parts of a similar geometry with this kitchen core. The result is slightly disorientating, abetted by visual distortions caused by the spiralling structure above. The railing, sometimes fine strands of steel cable evenly spaced below a larger, top segment, sometimes solid fir at the more perilous parts, allayed the clients' apprehension, especially for their child. The first run doubles back to a bridge, leading to the master bedroom suite to the left and, across the open living room below, to a pair of bedrooms, each with their own bathroom, and to a laundry room to the right. The effective use of a 'dumb-bell' plan at this level, in which the bridge across the double-height living room serves to link both ends of the linear

26

12

26 Wire guards are a safety feature on the railing on the bridge overlooking the living room.
27 Difficult geometries resulting in complex surfaces, such as this conference room at 8522 National Boulevard, have characterized Moss' work.
28 Rather than relying on conventional windows to provide light, Moss has provided clerestories that accentuate space and form, such as this long skylight in the master bedroom.
29 The clerestory window in the master bedroom continues on into the bathroom.

27

scheme, assures privacy as it turns the master suite into a small apartment of its own.

Once through the door leading into the master suite at its end of the bridge, a private world is revealed, contained by the long, sweeping western end wall of the house, where a custom-made double bed, with a continuous, overscaled sloping wooden headboard is situated. The curve of the wall puts it almost on axis with a fireplace cut into the thick service zone of the central cone opposite, with a built-in wood storage bin next to it. The roof of the bedroom slopes dramatically upwards from the curving end wall, making it seem tent-like, and an extended clerestory window between this roof and the vertical wall of the master bathroom encourages this impression. The window continues from the bedroom to the bathroom, making daylight and starlight available to both. This clerestory is indicative of Moss' attitude towards fenestration throughout the house, adding another layer of meaning to the broken

28

Palladian window facing the street (which is actually in the laundry room) as well as the deliberate precariousness and superficiality of the stock sash on the long southern elevation, and the trio of windows bent around the upper edge of the cone. Included as a significant part of his questioning of conventional 'inscription', Moss' preferred treatment is to allow light to accentuate form, with long slashing skylights placed in interstitial zones, while they are also at strategic positions above the central drum where the spiral unfolds.

The scale of the clerestory window in the bedroom is carefully controlled to accentuate a sense of intimacy; however the language the architect uses is the same, in which top light is clearly differentiated from light through windows in the wall. The privacy of the master suites, in stark contrast to the monumentality of the drum, is extended over onto a hidden, exterior balcony, accessible by a second door inside the main bridge entry. Complete with hot-tub

29

and conveniently located on top of the pantry projecting out from the kitchen below, which makes piping easier, the balcony looks down over the garden and is connected to it with a spiral stair, continuing the inside/outside balance expressed in the ground floor plan, at the clients' request.

Domestic *Carceri* Once outside this private realm, the encircling stair spiralling upwards in visual fragments inside the vertiginous cone generated by the kitchen, and the resulting diverse, omnidirectional perspectives, inevitably encourage comparisons with Piranesi, whether intentional or not on Moss' part. There are striking similarities that go beyond this most obvious analogy, related to Piranesi's reworking of his first, highly controversial series, under the second title of *Carceri d'invenzione*, in 1760.

30

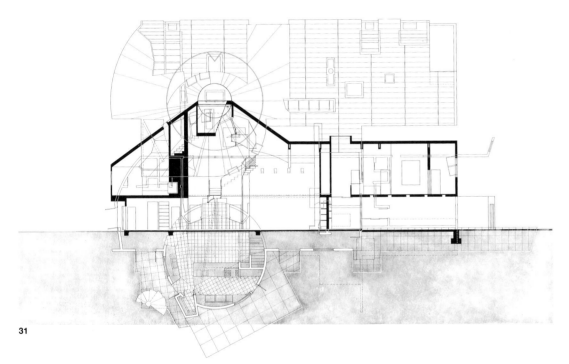

31

Originally conceived as a caprice and executed quickly on copper plates, Piranesi's first Prisons series, entitled *Invenzione capric di carceri*, were *scherzi* intended only for limited production. John Wilton-Ely has described these 14 plates as having 'constituted an experimental field of composition involving a sequence of brilliant improvisations on a limited set of themes … Careful study reveals a highly controlled discipline at work, exploiting the mechanics of Baroque illusionism through perspective and lighting to explore new dimensions of architectural expression.'[7] Deliberately conflicting sight lines and optical paradoxes heighten visual excitement, resulting in a mixture of expectation and frustration. As Wilton-Ely has said: 'each plate represents a powerful architectural experience itself whereby the entire Renaissance system of pictorial space is questioned with a degree of daring unparalleled before Cubism'.[8]

32

30 The vertiginous central core prompts comparisons with the soaring perspectives of Piranesi's *Carceri d'invenzione*, which seem to have several vanishing points.
31 Composite section/plan of the house.
32 Looking up into the central core is a dizzying visual experience as bridges, stairs and structural elements seem to fly in all directions.

Piranesi's *Carceri d'invenzione* which followed 15 years later were prompted by polemic attacks made on Baroque architecture, and implicitly on Italian sensibilities, by nascent rationalists such as Laugier and Blondel. Extending his earlier themes of paradox and the manipulation of spatial perception in a deliberate attempt to create confusion, Piranesi takes the *Carceri* to a higher level as an attack on the rigidity of convention. This is expressed through monumentality, contrast, amplified formal expression, theatricality, and the predominance of structure presented by staircases, extended bridges, galleries and precarious roofs seemingly without end. Characterized by John Wilton-Ely as 'melodramas', implying the representation of extravagant emotion, this new series, beyond its nationalistic overtones, was an artistic affirmation of a belief in empiricism in favour of logic and mysticism instead of systematic proof.

14

33 Offset centroids contribute to
the spatial excitement of the
house's central core, but also
made it difficult to build.
34–36 A series of views of study
models clarifies the relationship
of various elements of the house,
showing the elevation facing the
side garden (34), the street
entrance (35) and the central
core without its sloping roof (36).

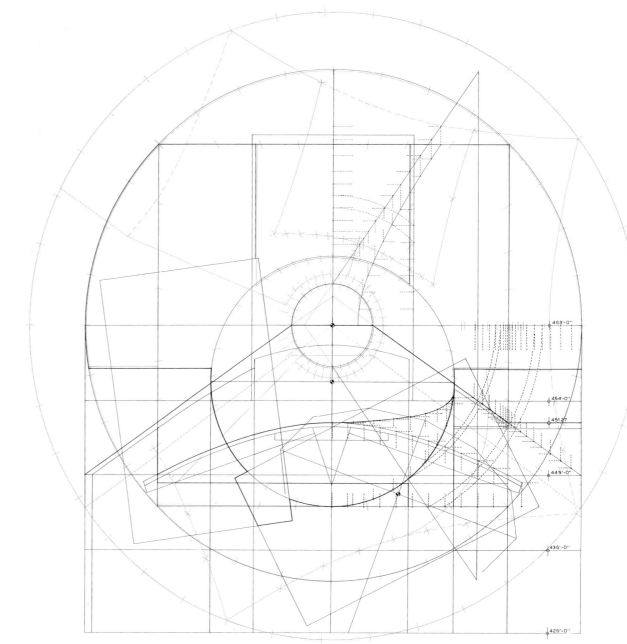

33

34

35

36

Piranesi's challenge to the predictable monocentric expectation of architectural space initi-ated by Brunelleschi in the technique of one point perspective is germane to the Lawson-Westen House since Eric Owen Moss has used this design to update the same argument. While other art forms have adapted to polycentrism, through Cubism in art, or stochastic polyphony in music, architecture has remained tied to a monocular perspectival vision, in spite of contravening efforts by Bernini and others. The shift that has taken place since Piranesi drew the *Carceri d'invenzione*, brought about by the electronic abstraction of our perception of reality, has forced the issue, leading Moss to attempt what he has termed 'a conceptual dissection' of the physical fabric at various scales in order to alter the mechanics of vision and mental orientation. The kitchen cone, with its fractured stair to nowhere (or to a crows' nest overlooking the entire region from the mountains to the Pacific Ocean, to be more

37

37 An exhilarating view of abstract forms in the exterior spiral stairway.
38 The fractured and bent 'Venturi window' can be read as an analogy for social change.
39 The house extends to cover an outdoor whirlpool bath on a balcony outside the master bedroom, and a spiral stairway, which leads down to the garden.

38

precise), is the major focus of that alteration, methodically diverting the customary process of optical rationalization at every turn. In its place, the architect has substituted a novel peda-gogy of structure which implies rather than reinforces space, and a chaotic order, which ini-tially appears to be illogical.

De-centring the ideas of House This process is then carried through, at a smaller scale, to the syntax of construction so that each element with traditional associations is questioned and the typology is pulled apart, to detach, as Peter Eisenman has said, 'what one sees from what one knows – the eye from the mind'.[9]

In positing another way of seeing, which he calls 'looking back', in order to differentiate it from the traditional expectations of straightforward monocular perspective, Eisenman has

also noted that it would be necessary, following this detachment which may be equated with the refraction Moss has achieved in the kitchen cone, to inscribe space differently. As Eisen-man has stated: 'All architecture can be said to be already inscribed. Windows, doors, beams and columns are a kind of inscription. These make architecture know, they reinforce vision. Since no space is uncircumscribed, we do not see a window without relating it to an idea of window, this kind of inscription seems not only natural but necessary to architecture.'[10]

The skewed window on the forward concrete wall facing the street, which acts as a signal of Moss' intention to reinscribe familiar associations, has been deliberately bisected and is repeated in its normal configuration in an adjoining wall to reiterate its brokenness, through rotation. The similarity of the size and shape of this window, when mentally reassembled, to another on the Vanna Venturi House, as well as Moss' disclaimer that his multi-directional

39

front door is not 'a Venturi joke', both prompt a provocative line of speculative comparison, since the role of fenestration as a sign in each instance is similar. But the basic motivation of each architect is completely different, tracing an important shift in social values. In his mother's house in 1963, Robert Venturi provided a built example of the 'decorated shed' – the separation of the facade as a signifier from the functional body of the house – in order to break away from the Modernist canon of formalism. Taking one step further Louis Kahn's concept of layering, introduced in his United States Consulate project in Luanda, Angola (1959) for environmental reasons, so that it becomes a means of cultural commentary, Venturi has used the 'inscriptions' that Eisenman has identified as a code for 'houseness' to reinforce rather than destroy the concept of domesticity, albeit in an ironic way. As the literal representation of what Venturi believed to be 'a child's idea of a house', at least in the western hemisphere, the front

40

16

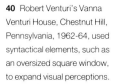

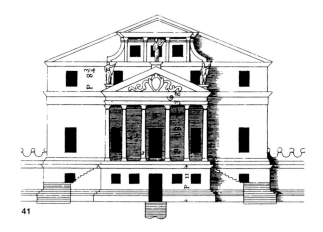

41

screen wall and its component parts are all loaded with messages related to perceived continuities and changes in the residence as an institution. On that facade, which could be seen as a billboard advertising the history of the house on the east coast of North America in abbreviated code, many references are excluded in spite of its reputed inclusivity. What *is* whimsically included, beginning the Post-Modern penchant for acontextual historicism, is a parallel reference to Andrea Palladio, because of Venturi's equivalent passion for Renaissance architecture. As the first to embrace the notion of attaching a temple front to a villa, thereby combining the secular with the sacred and raising the status of the house to a quasi-religious object, Palladio also helped to codify the transfer from classically derived, geometric proportion used in the Middle Ages, to the arithmetic obsessions of the Renaissance in his *I Quattro Libri dell'Architettura* of 1570. This treatise, as well as the grid system used in his villa designs

and contrary to a commonly held belief, glorified the square over the golden section, showing a preference for rational rather than irrational numbers.[11] This preference is substantiated by the figure studies of Leonardo da Vinci in *De Divina Proportione* of 1609, which relate human proportions to a circle and a square after the constituent divisions, due also to previous associations. As Rudolf Wittkower has described these: 'The square or cube, the right-angle isosceles triangle (the diagonal of the square), the pentagon – all these figures were charged by Plato with deep and even mystic significance. I think it is due to the emotional importance attached to them by the Greek mind that these geometrical forms had an extraordinary influence on the European conception of proportion.'[12]

Venturi subtly conveys the substance of this theoretical shift, from Medieval divine proportion to the anthropomorphism of the Renaissance, through a deceptively simple sequence of

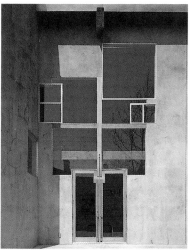

42

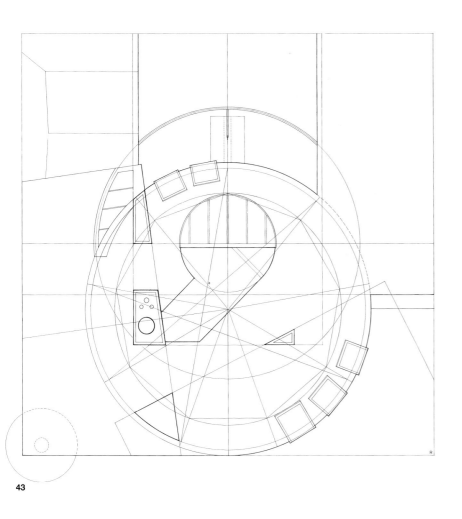

43

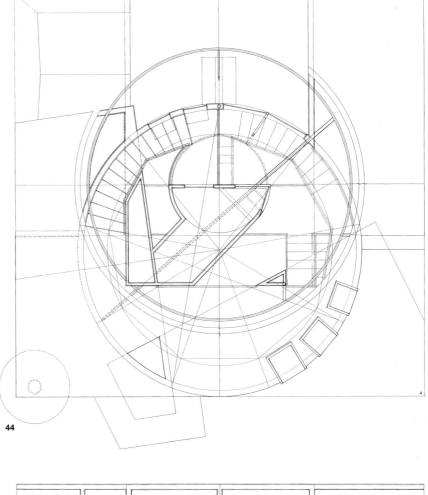

44

43–45 Planar cuts through various progressive levels of the central core, help to convey the directional shift that occurs towards the top.

46, 47 The spiral stair adjacent to the core continues the circular motion of the main interior stair into the exterior garden space.

46

47

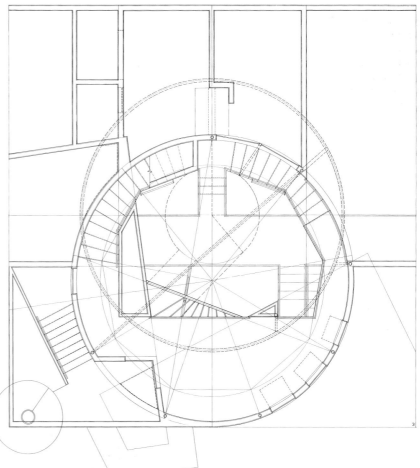

45

signs, such as a pedimented front manneristically broken into two triangles, an oversized square entrance inscribed within an implied circle, and a square Palladian window anchoring it all, while also managing to evoke McKim Mead and White. The outrageously large window bisected into four parts by mullions which are also pressed into semiotic duty as a reminder of the Renaissance preference for a centrally planned Greek cross Church, as pedantically presented as one of Serlio's typologies, is deliberately placed to get attention, being much closer to the end of the facade than one would normally expect, with its sill at ground level. Yet, regardless of its more arcane historical connotations it glorifies rather than questions the sanctity of the domicile, just as the temple front does, with the sign for a dado leading to it just to reinforce the point. By bringing something normally associated with the lower third of an interior wall to an exaggerated position on this front facade, the messages for inside and out-

48

18

49

side are mixed. While it may be argued that the lower sill of the Palladian window combined with this inside-out wall confuses traditional boundaries and exposes what has always been protected, the impression these divergent parts convey is overwhelming.

The blatant, four-square Palladian window in Chestnut Hill and its shattered aluminium counterpart in Brentwood, as well as the facades they explicate, are equally perceptive analogies of their respective times. Separated by 30 years and 2,000 miles, they describe a radical change in the idea of home which Robert Venturi and Denise Scott Brown, however, contentiously defend as still remaining intact.[13] Contemporaneous with the death of President John F Kennedy, the Vanna Venturi House marks the end of a period of high optimism in America, as well as two decades of its greatest influence after World War II. Those halcyon years were followed in rapid succession by a sequence of depressing episodes: Vietnam;

50

Watergate; terrorism and humiliation in Iran; race riots, the painful shift from an industrial to an information-based economy; pollution (the official denial of which culminated in governmental refusal to acknowledge the Rio Summit); unemployment; homelessness; and crime. The sociological symptoms of the changes that have taken place in America (but which are not exclusive to it) include decreasing salaries, a decimated middle class, soaring divorce rates, an increase in non-nuclear families, rising real estate prices, and diminished expectations.

The dilemma that Moss has chosen to confront, then, is how to embody these fundamental changes in a house for a couple that does not necessarily exemplify them, but by still remaining faithful to the clients' brief. To do so he has chosen to exaggerate congruencies, clearly separate from divergent commentary.

Home is a relatively new idea To clarify where those points specifically occur in this building, and how they have been adjusted to relate to social context, it will be helpful to trace briefly the comparatively recent concept of 'home' and how it has evolved. Although closely associated with physical and mental comfort in the contemporary developed world, which recognizes that a house is not always classified in this category if it doesn't provide both, the idea of home was not always so clearly defined. In the fourteenth century, particularly in Europe, protection and communication of status took precedence over privacy and ease, with functions allocated in ways that are totally alien to us today. Witold Rybczynski, who has noted that the word comfortable comes from the Latin root word *confortare* meaning to strengthen, has said: 'The typical bourgeois town house of the fourteenth century combined living and work … These long narrow buildings usually consisted of two floors over an undercroft, or base-

51

51 The whirlpool bath, on a raised platform outside the master bedroom, is positioned to allow complete privacy and yet have a view towards the garden below.

52 Rather than using a conventional change in materials for the roof of the central core, the architect has continued to use the coloured stucco that covers the side walls, for continuity.

53 The view downwards to the garden, from the outside whirlpool bath.

52

ment, which was used for storage. The main floor of the house, or at least that part that faced the street, was a shop … The living quarters were not, as we would expect, a series of rooms; instead, they consisted of a single large chamber – the hall – which was open up to the rafters. People cooked, ate, entertained and slept in this space.'[14] These homes, which were frequently crowded and minimally furnished were not without their compensations, but do demonstrate that, as Rybczynski says: 'There was no awareness of comfort as an objective idea.'[15] Such a distinction was only to come later, in the seventeenth century, particularly in Dutch painting which captured a mood of interior intimacy and exemplified by such painters as Vermeer, de Witte and Franz Hals. Through these artists' work, the house took on an exhalted stature as a nurturing place providing both protection and delight. As the source of sustenance within it, the kitchen began to be especially revered, while compartmentalized as

53

a private realm. From Holland the historical, physical and ideological distance to the English country house is small, and from the seventeenth to the early twentieth century, the concept of domestic comfort was refined even further in English architecture. In that time, furnishing especially began to play a more significant and highly specialized role. No longer designed to satisfy rudimentary, functional needs or to convey status as medieval furniture did, interior accoutrements became more integral with the individual spaces they occupied, eventually leading, through the influence of Charles Rennie and Margaret Macdonald Mackintosh, to the idea of a room as a unified 'total work of art'.

The process of simplification, stemming from the Arts and Crafts reaction to Victorian clutter, which the Mackintoshes themselves accelerated, was adopted as an article of faith by the Modern Movement, due also in no small part to Hermann Muthesius' *Das Englische Haus.* In all, the chronology of this transformation, from the objectification of the idea of domestic comfort at the beginning of the Bourgeois age to its final rationalization by Le Corbusier, was to occupy little more than three hundred years, with parallels in America that have an even shorter time line. As one of the final paradigms of that tradition, assembled from shingle-style variants bred in New England, the Vanna Venturi house continues to reflect the increasing desire for privacy that was an important part of it, particularly in the compartmentalized kitchen. Still implying familial stereotypes that were just beginning to be seriously questioned when it was built, this kitchen also derives from a time when domestic help, meant to be as unobtrusive as possible, was taken for granted above a certain social level.

In the Gamble House, Pasadena, which predates the Lawson-Westen House by 86 years, the extensive kitchen at the heart of the plan, which was intentionally insulated from the rooms

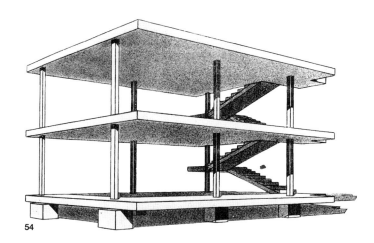

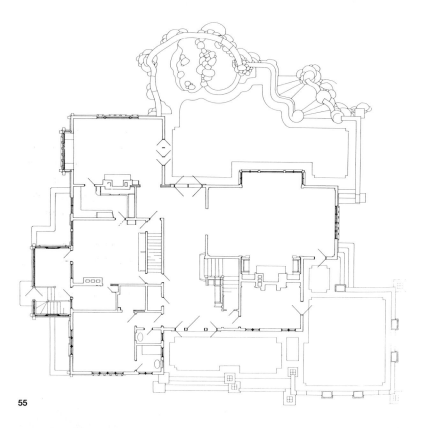

55

around it by a buffer of various utilitarian spaces to muffle the noise of food preparation, was the domain of 'the girls', as the three women who served the family were known. An elaborate system of pulleys and bells connected to a control panel, as well as hidden sliding doors and an unobtrusive back entrance for deliveries, were also added to the kitchen to ensure that this aspect of domestic comfort, at least, remained discreetly separate from the rest.

The main thrust of the Case Study programme, initiated by John Entenza in Los Angeles shortly after World War II, was in fact established to encourage local architects to submit designs for 'the servantless house'. It was to be representative of the less formal living patterns that Entenza correctly anticipated returning GIs would demand, and the plans he published typically promoted more open interiors, and a blurred distinction between inside and outside space. Following prototypes such as the Barnsdall House and Rudolf Schindler's res-

54 Le Corbusier's Maison Dom-Ino structural system was intended to apply mass production techniques to housing.
55 The Gamble House kitchen was buffered by surrounding spaces to prevent noise infiltration into the other parts of the house.
56 Charles and Ray Eames' Eames House, Pacific Palisades, 1949, reflected changing social patterns in America following World War II.

idence on King's Road, based on a balance between internal zones and external landscaped courts, the Case Study entries addressed a public eager for a more casual lifestyle. While there are still distinct rooms in the Eames House, for example, which was one of the early submissions in this programme, they are less obvious and the kitchen is especially indicative of this trend.

56

Congruencies and divergence With this background in mind, particularly as it relates to recent changes in residential design in Southern California, it becomes possible to identify those parts of the Lawson-Westen House which concur with changing patterns as well as Moss' epistolary brief, and those which relate to wider social issues not necessarily connected with the clients who wrote it.

The spiralling series of spaces at the heart of the Lawson-Westen House, each relating to a natural external equivalent, are in the best tradition of the region with the increasing tendency towards internal openness an obvious continuity. The kitchen at the hub of these spaces also follows that pattern, with a significant difference, partly related to gender determinacy and partly to the harsh realities of life in Los Angeles in almost equal measure. The buffer of rooms and service areas surrounding it may make it seem generically similar to the same areas in the Gamble House, in spite of configuration and technological advances, and yet the intention behind the space has altered radically.

Once considered solely a woman's domain and refuge, the kitchen has now become a place where work is shared, and where guests are also welcome. Food preparation has been elevated from backbreaking labour performed out of sight in a hot, soundproof room, to high

57

57–59 The openness of the Lawson-Westen kitchen reflects the change that has taken place in contemporary residences, in which food preparation has become a participatory activity.

58

art with a new set of rituals, supported by the rationale that everyone always ends up in the kitchen and it is more comfortable there. The food revolution that began in America, led by Julia Child, Craig Claiborne and James Beard, and occurring at about the same time as the social upheaval that Moss addresses in his design, spawned a burgeoning industry of its own, with an increasingly sophisticated following that began to insist on higher standards in restaurants and to demonstrate confidence in cooking skills by having elaborate dinner parties at home.

As with most trends in America, Los Angeles led the way in this – albeit with strong competition from New York – where a majority of the gastronomic mentors and the publishers who promoted them are based. 'California Cuisine' began to capture the high ground in the food war between the two cities in the mid-seventies, with Wolfgang Puck and his wife Barbara

59

Lazaroff proving to be inspired tacticians in the campaign by opening up the kitchens in their various, wildly successful restaurants to public view. This reinforced the idea of cooking as a performance in a city which already regards most other aspects of life in that way; where reality is substantiated by artifice, rather than a determinant of it. In the fragmented city of Los Angeles that has no centre and with the significant increase in the amount of violent crime, restaurants with secure valet parking have now become important social institutions, regardless of how frivolous they may seem to non-Angelenos, as places where people prefer to meet for business, pleasure or both. That same rising crime rate, however, and the paranoia induced by writers who have capitalized on it, such as Mike Davis and Seth Morgan, have increasingly led to a bunker mentality, manifested in a growing reluctance to leave home after dark.

21

An appropriate metaphor Piranesi's *Carceri* does not equate with the liberated Lawson-Westen kitchen, but Moss moves from coincidental consent with his clients' brief to broader social commentary in the structure of the drum above it. Many in Los Angeles now willingly incarcerate themselves in their houses after dark, their self-imposed sentences in direct proportion to material wealth and property. Thus the faux metallic steel-trowelled plaster shell of the house may also be read as a symptom of this pervasive fortress mentality – but again, as with everything else in Los Angeles, appearances can be deceiving. Continuing the intriguing, many-layered comparison with the Vanna Venturi house, which was intentionally built to look like an architectural model both out of whimsy and pedagogical thoroughness, to underscore the purpose of the decorated shed, the Lawson-Westen House also resembles its model, but for different reasons. While describing the three-dimensional studies of close competitor

60

61

22

62

60, 61 The difference between the long elevation facing the garden and its opposite indicates the tight site constraints that Moss had to deal with. Study models all have a metallic aspect.
62 The continuous roof surface of the central core of the house adds to the impression of monumentality.
63 When the continuity of the exterior surface is broken, it usually occurs in the least conspicuous areas.

63

Thom Mayne, Fritz Neumeyer might just as easily have been describing those that fill Moss' office when he said that: 'Models appear with a patina and colouring that evokes the impression of the monolithic, as if they were objects cast in bronze or some other dense metal. In this aesthetic of proudly hand-worked surfaces, there is reflected a longing supressed into the architectonic subconscious, a longing for an "architecturalness of the object" saturated with the monumentality of form, weight of significance, and authenticity of being.'[16] Carried over into the steel-trowelled, pigmented plaster surface of the house, this wish to convey an impression of monumentality is clearly differentiated from the concrete segment with the fragmented window facing the street and the final emphatic sentence of the concurring and diverging dialogue, clearly accentuated by the absence of sills on the exterior surface. The plaster is carried up and over the central drum, replacing a conventional roof as another major

alteration of a universally recognized item of inscription; and so the need for an image of permanence in a city where change has the highest value is given precedence over the most elemental sign for 'home'.

De Man, not Decon: a third commentary Given the increasing rapidity with which stylistic attributions come and go and the difficulty involved in categorizing any of the most avant-garde Los Angeles architects (let alone in grouping them together as part of a 'School'), it would be a hasty generalization to identify Eric Owen Moss as a 'deconstructivist', or to point to the Lawson-Westen House as further evidence of any tendencies in that direction. When questioned on this point, Moss confesses to a keener interest in the writings of Paul de Man than Jacques Derrida. The difference is instructive of important aspects of his design philosophy and the place that the house occupies within it.

Unlike Derrida, whom he met in 1966 when he was 57 and had already formulated many of his ideas, Paul de Man sought to develop a terminology that coincided with the structure of language and a rhetorical means by which to examine a text, rather than a 'metalanguage' by which to destroy it.[17] Lindsay Waters has described the difference by saying that: 'Some understand de Man's work since 1968 by reference to the ideas of Derrida and what has come to be called deconstruction, but this is inadequate … Derrida has, I think, little direct influence of de Man beyond what he says in the key suggestive pages at the beginning of *The White Mythology* on the materiality of the "inscription" … To subsume de Man under the rubric of deconstruction is misleading.'[18]

While he and Derrida have both concentrated on an exegesis of the same philosophical tradition, which in itself tends to be self-referential, de Man has taken particular exception to Hei-

64–66 An early sketch series, showing how the basic concept and spatial geometry of the house was derived.

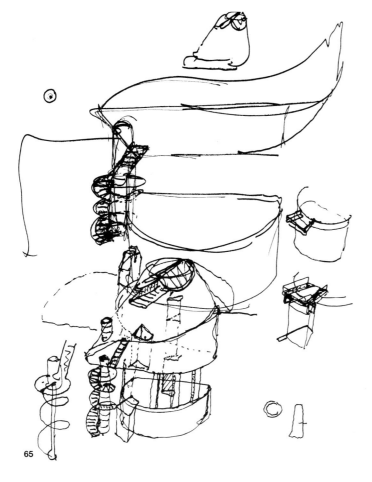

65

64

degger's interpretation of the poet and novelist Hölderlin, providing one key reason why the label is inappropriate to him and also, by extension, to Moss. Paul de Man differs with Heidegger at the point at which Heidegger interprets Hölderlin as having equated 'Nature' with 'the Law', since, as a follower of Hölderlin, de Man does not agree with this equation.[19]

The alternative to natural law, in the linear, Newtonian sense, is chaos, which contemporary physicists now use as the name for a competing theory, based on the study of seemingly random behaviour and the extreme sensitivity to, instead of a predictable dependence on original conditions. Rather than producing completely erratic results, however, as first suspected, chaos theory is increasingly being seen as the foundation of a new kind of order, rather than the absence of it, behaving with a complex logic of its own. Like de Man, Moss attempts to question the conventional, accepted idea of order and ideological expectation and tries to

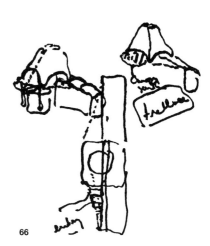

66

discover a different logic, in a *constructive* rather than nihilistic way. The one point of agreement between Derrida and de Man, regarding the materiality of the 'inscription', is also important, in that their consensus on text, appropriated by Peter Eisenman in reference to architectural elements, carries over to what Moss has identified as 'a general operational principle' in his work, of questioning the conventional identity of those elements as part of an ideology. Regarding the Lawson-Westen House, as he has said, 'one could conceivably reconstitute the geometry using the constituent components of the house and return to several recognizable pieces. Pieces were removed. So some parts are literal, some theoretical. You don't get the geometric totality immediately, but by implication. It can be derived intellectually. But experientially, the space has no total'.[20] Moss focuses on what de Man saw as the promise inherent in language, in the new inscription he creates through that implication rather than attacking its weaknesses, so leaving it disconnected, fragmented and illegible.

Telltale clues such as diagrams of Lorenz attractors in the corner of sketches of the Lawson-Westen House to the contrary, Moss' awareness of chaos theory and its relationship to deconstruction has not prevented him from adopting a more sympathetic stance. The real significance of his allegiance to de Man is that he shares a similar view seeing the undiscovered order in chaos theory as vital and potentially good, rather than simply dangerous; a theoretical construct analogous to nature itself.

In this way Moss and the house he has designed align with theories that are far more venerable than those reconstructed to take advantage of a passing fad. Their genealogy predates Anaxagoras, originating in the eastern philosophies to which Moss frequently refers. His interpretations of dynamic balance, continuous motion and inevitable change, in combination with

67

68

67 Henry Moore, *Helmet Head No 2*, 1950, bronze, height 34.3cm. Moore's Helmet series was an important source of inspiration for Moss, depicting the fragile quality of the human condition and the protection provided by artificial constructs.
68, 69 The architectural armour that Moss has provided for his clients has few gaps, but when they do occur they provide an enticing hint of the contrasting luxury inside the house.

69

the concept of the whole represented in the fractal enlargement of its most minuscule part, are all evident in his work, but are subservient to a more humanistic agenda. This is particularly expressed in the creature comforts of the Lawson-Westen House completed at the brink of the 'post-theory' period, in which a general disenchantment with post-structuralism has put the emphasis back on language once again; with the house a figurative bridge between the liberating, but ultimately nihilistic, act of disjuncture symbolized by deconstruction, and a new initiative towards social communication.

Regardless of other readings, one of the major sources of inspiration that the architect himself admits to is the 'Helmet Series' of sculptures by Henry Moore, characterized by thick, semi-circular bronze shells wrapped around a dendritic centre – a sensitive depiction of the source of human intelligence, shielded from harm by a protective construct. In contemporary

Los Angeles, which is generally categorized as being a social barometer for the rest of a nation that consistently looks to it for new trends, the awareness of potential harm seems to be missing, with the debate carried out in the media centring around the question of public paranoia. While sociologists continue to discuss the extent to which such fear may be disproportionate – or not – architects must grapple with clients' perceptions of danger in a city that is a petri dish of cultural experimentation and racial mixtures. Eric Owen Moss has chosen to use the Lawson-Westen commission as a commentary on those perceptions. The dominant drum at the centre of the house speaks to a similar, most basic instinct: the preservation of the best and most fragile parts of a cultural legacy – an intention which has historically been behind all great architecture.

Photographs

The architect has used the entrance elevation facing Westgate Avenue as a means of projecting several of the basic ideas used in the design of the house, yet without revealing too much. The most significant of these is that of the bisected, square window, dislocated from its original, orthogonal position, and seeming to have been broken in the process. The shape of the concrete portal frame also reflects the roof structure of the living room behind it.

Moss typically pays a great deal of attention to detailing the main entrances into his buildings, attempting to make each one singularly original. This has now evolved into a sophisticated game, intended to change commonly held perceptions of what doors should look like, and the dimension in which they should exist. He delights in changing the rules of that game by turning solid into void, front into back, the usual into the unusual, and the main entrance of the Lawson-Westen House continues this process.

The side entrance from the garden is used as an additional opportunity to comment on what Peter Eisenman has described as 'inscription', or the impression usually conveyed by the parts of a building that we take for granted. In this abstract assemblage, Moss has placed such parts in an ususual composition, as if putting them on display for reassessment, placing them in conditions they would not normally be seen in to arouse curiosity about their absence throughout the rest of the house.

The unconventional roof form of the core of the house, with the steel ring beam of its circumference partly exposed, is the result of the interlocking geometries Moss has used, intentionally unlike the expected semiotic symbol for shelter. Consistent with the architect's handling of constructional elements elsewhere, it draws habitual assumptions into question, offering an alternative way of seeing. The results are compositionally engaging, disturbing and undeniably memorable.

The unexpected juxtaposition of an angular corner and a metal railing, seen when looking up into the core, is typical of many such spatial surprises found throughout the house. The contrast of materials and textures provided by these intersections is a constant source of visual delight.

The metal fireplace in the living room, with its exposed chimney, serrated bookcases and lintel-like projection over the door leading to the main entrance, was conceived as a sculptural object that qualifies the enormous scale of the space. A collaborative design with its fabricator, it is representative of Moss' commitment to total aesthetic control.

Looking towards the living room and its fireplace from the kitchen, the view is framed by the changing angles of the main stair to the upper level of the house. The contrast between hard and soft materials is most pronounced in these two major spaces, with various kinds of metal offset by the tactile richness of wooden cabinets.

The kitchen, designed in close collaboration with the clients, is literally and symbolically the heart of the house, strategically located to provide views in all directions. Its requirements generated the original concept, which altered surprisingly little as the scheme evolved.

Unlike the spaces around it, the dining room conveys an impression of serenity, with a ceiling height that approximates residential convention. Much of the clients' extensive art collection is located here, since it is a self-contained area that makes it possible to concentrate on each piece displayed. Considered to be an extension of the kitchen, the dining room is scaled to encourage appreciation of the food that guests have watched being prepared – or have helped to prepare – and the conversation that accompanies it.

The vertiginous central stair which inevitably draws comparisons with Piranesi's *Carceri d'invenzione*, due to the multiple perspectives that it offers. The stair alternatively penetrates into the soaring space above it, and then protrudes outwards from it, in a complex compositional strategy which draws the eye inexorably upwards. The thin, vertically articulated space stands in sharp contrast to the broad expanse of living room wall next to it.

Framed views are used by Moss as opportunities for visual collage of wood, metal and stucco which seem to appear around every corner. Some are arguably coincidental; many, however, are not, and are the final result of a painstaking series of models built at a scale large enough to study such juxtapositions – and control them. Frequently, the models focused only on details, analysing each in enlarged isolation, as well as in relation to sequencing.

46

Structural bracing in the main stair core, the look of heavy metal tempered by the soft colour of the walls that are penetrated by the interlocking frame. Such assemblages regularly intercept vertical movement up the stair, giving the impression of sequential progression through gateways, on the way from the public to the private realm of the house.

Location plan

1 Lawson-Westen House

Sunset Boulevard

Foxboro Drive

Westgate Avenue

1

Kearsarge Street

0   200m

0   200yds

Location plan

Drawings

Site plan

1 Lawson-Westen House
2 driveway
3 concrete walkway
4 landscaping
5 wall planters
6 bench

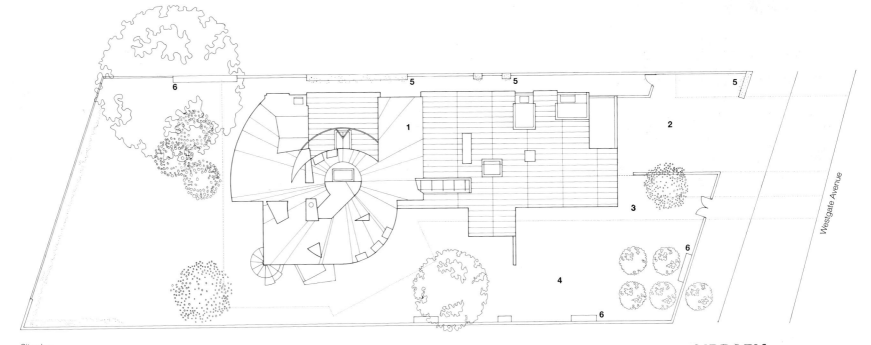

6   5   5   5

1   2

3

6

4   6

Westgate Avenue

0   5m

0   15ft

Site plan

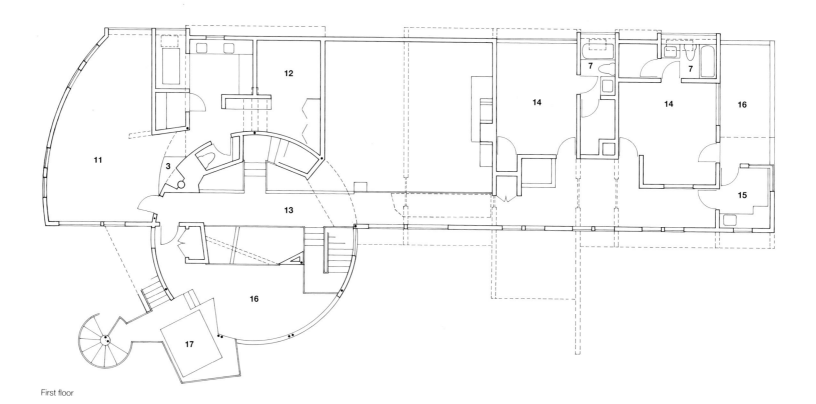

First floor

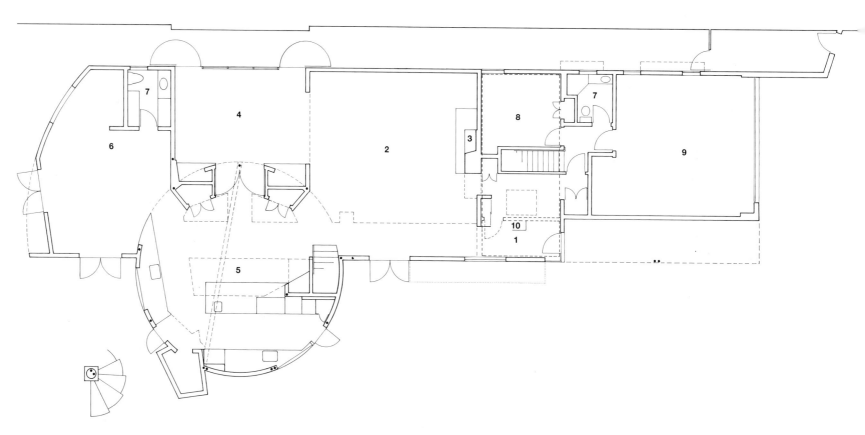

0   3m

0   10ft

Ground floor

Floor plans

1 entrance hall
2 living room
3 fireplace
4 dining room
5 kitchen
6 family room
7 bathroom
8 guest room
9 garage
10 basement and wine cellar
11 master bedroom
12 dressing room
13 bridge
14 bedroom
15 laundry
16 deck
17 jacuzzi
18 mezzanine
19 roof deck

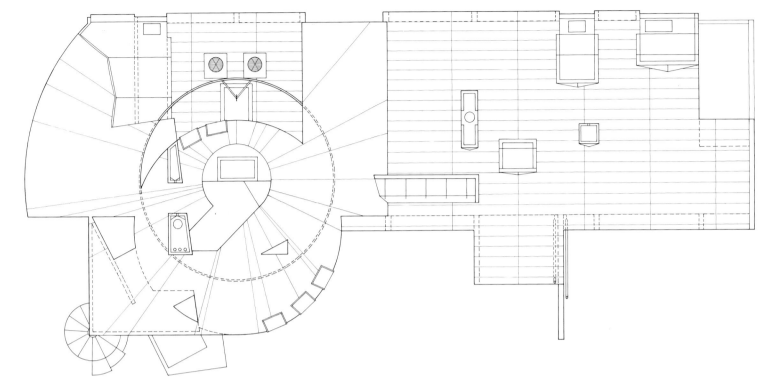

Roof

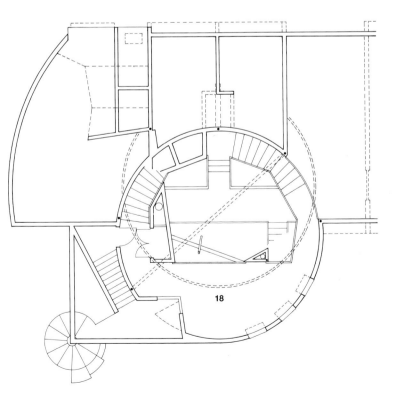

Mezzanine

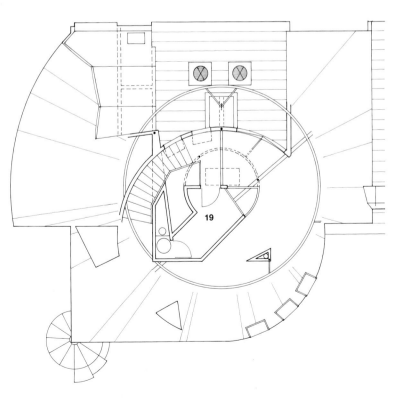

Mechanical roof

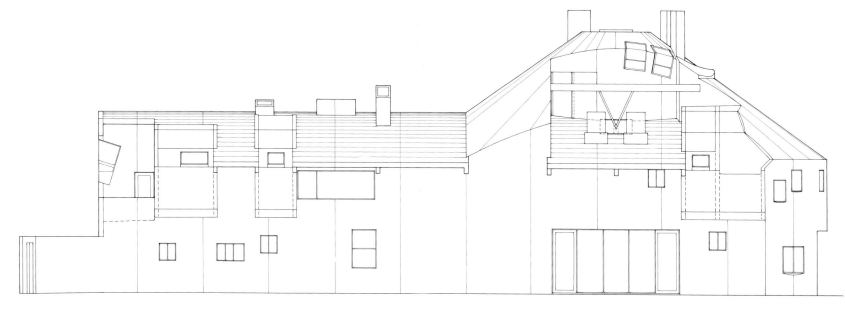

North elevation

South elevation

West elevation

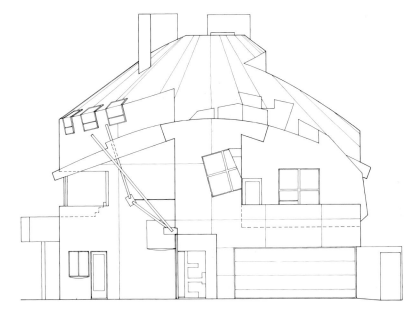

East elevation

Sections

1 entrance hall
2 living room
3 kitchen
4 family room
5 master bedroom
6 laundry
7 basement
8 bedroom
9 deck
10 dining room
11 bridge
12 bathroom
13 mezzanine
14 roof deck
15 dressing room
16 garage

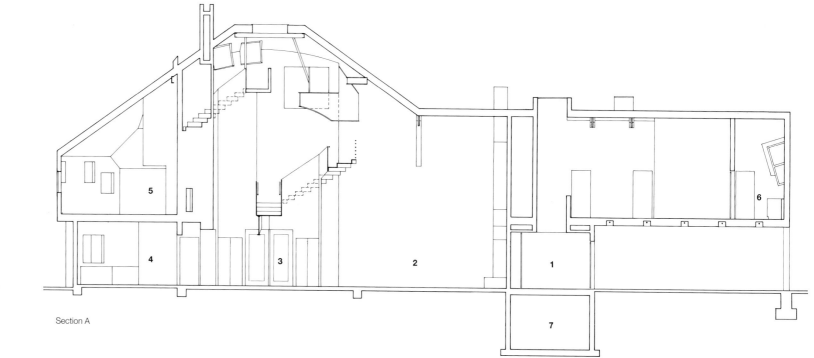

Section A

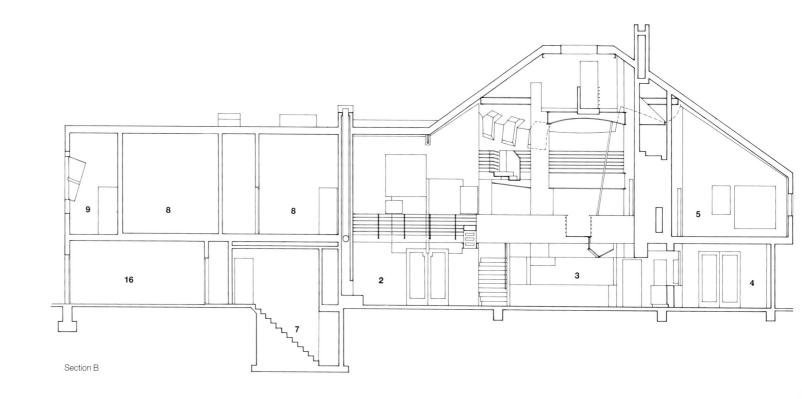

Section B

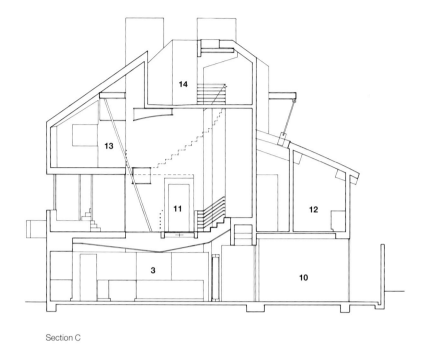

Section C

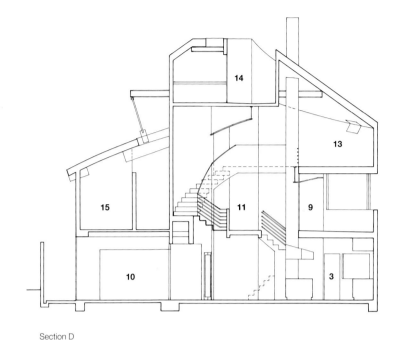

Section D

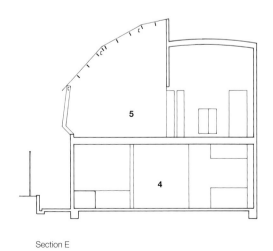

Section E

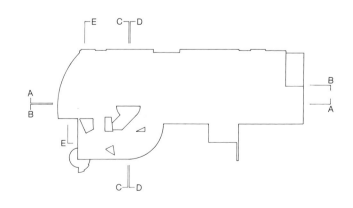

56   **Axonometric of structural mullion**

1 ½in (12.7mm) steel mullion
2 ¼in (6.3mm) steel flange
3 ½2in (12.7mm) steel spacer
4 ¼in (6.3mm) anchor plate
   (concealed)
5 ¼in (6.3mm) jamb welded
   to mullion
6 ⅜in (9.5mm) spacer welded
   to mullion/jamb
7 ¼in (6.3mm) cover plate
8 ⅜in (7.9mm) laminated
   glass
9 machine bolts
10 sloping plasterboard cill
11 plasterboard lining
12 metal cill flashing
13 silicon seal
14 roof waterproofing

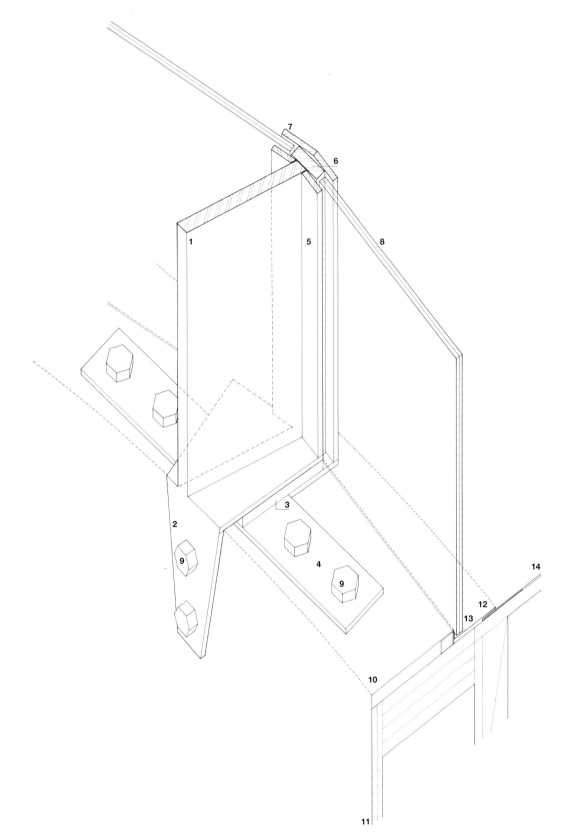

Axonometric view at C

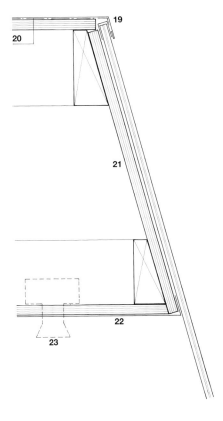

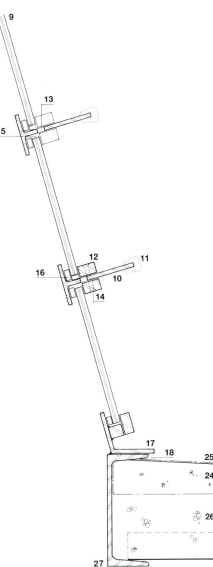

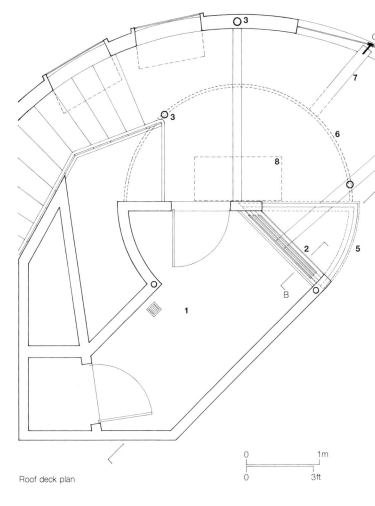

Roof deck plan

0   1m
0   3ft

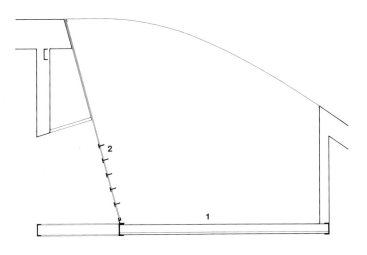

Section A

0   100mm
0   4ins

Clerestory sloping window   57

1   mechanical roof
2   sloping clerestory window
3   circular steel column
4   steel girder
5   6 x 13in (152 x 330 mm) steel channel
6   steel channel above
7   steel strut
8   skylight above
9   ⁵⁄₁₆in (7.9mm) tempered laminated glass
10   steel T mullion
11   rubber extrusion
12   steel glass stop
13   ½in (12.7mm) diameter hole
14   countersunk machine screw
15   silicon caulking
16   vinyl setting block
17   ³⁄₁₆in (4.8mm) steel plate cill
18   caulking
19   galvanized sheet metal flashing
20   asphaltic paper waterproofing
21   ⅝in (15.9mm) plywood
22   galvanized sheet metal soffit
23   light fitting
24   1½in (38mm) concrete topping
25   elastomeric waterproofing
26   3in (76.2mm) structural concrete slab on metal deck
27   steel channel

Hyperbolic roof

1 galvanized sheet metal roofing on asphalt felt
2 plywood (x2)
3 2x10in (50.8 x 254 mm) timber joists
4 plasterboard (x2)
5 2in (50.4mm) wide inverted U beam from ⅜in (9.5mm) steel plate
6 8¾in (222.25mm) laminated timber beam
7 timber/plywood framing
8 ⅞in (22.2mm) cement render on lath
9 plasterboard
10 steel channel
11 ⅝in (15.9mm) diameter steel strut
12 ⅝in (15.9mm) diameter steel tie rod
13 glass
14 timber plate
15 stiffeners in inverted U beam
16 1¼in (31.7mm) diameter machine bolts
17 ½in (12.7mm) steel plate
18 # 2 clevis
19 light fitting
20 steel angle fixing welded to strut
21 carpet
22 1½in (38mm) lightweight concrete
23 2x1½in (38mm) lightweight concrete

58

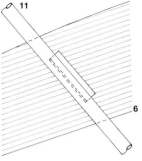

Detail C

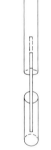

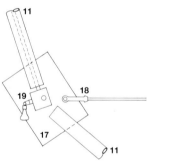

Detail B

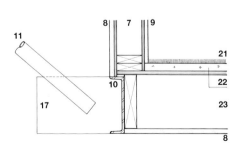

Detail A

Detail D

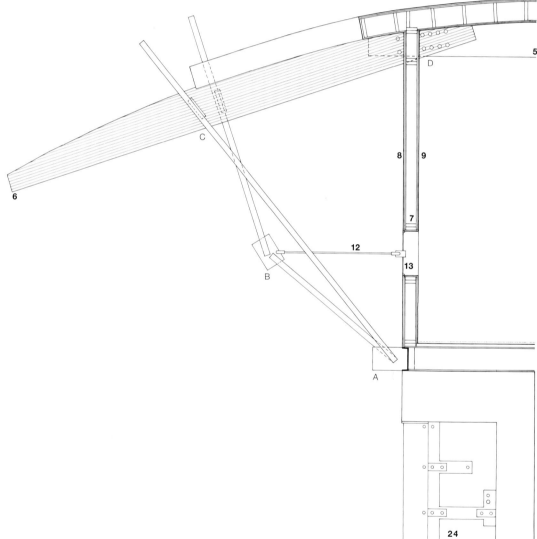

Roof and wall section

0   200mm

0   8ins

0   1m

0   3ft

Front door

1. ½in (12.7mm) tempered glass door
2. 1¾in (44.5mm) mahogany
3. concealed dowel
4. ¼in (6.3mm) steel plate hot rolled
5. ⅝in (15.9mm) machine bolts
6. cylinder dead bolt
7. cylinder lockset
8. hinge
9. ⅛in (3.2mm) aluminium strike box
10. offset top pivot
11. offset floor pivot
12. ⅜in (9.5mm) tempered glass window
13. aluminium glazing frame
14. 2in (50.8mm) polished concrete topping
15. aluminium angle threshold
16. 20 gauge metal flashing
17. exterior concrete
18. plywood
19. timber/plywood framing
20. door shoe
21. 1¾in (44.5mm) diameter steel washer
22. 1¾in (44.5mm) diameter neoprene washer
23. 2x2in (50.8x50.8mm) steel washer
24. 2x2in (50.8x50.8mm) neoprene washer
25. cement render on lath
26. ⅝in (15.9mm) plasterboard
27. caulking
28. silicon mitre corner

59

Detail E

Plan   C

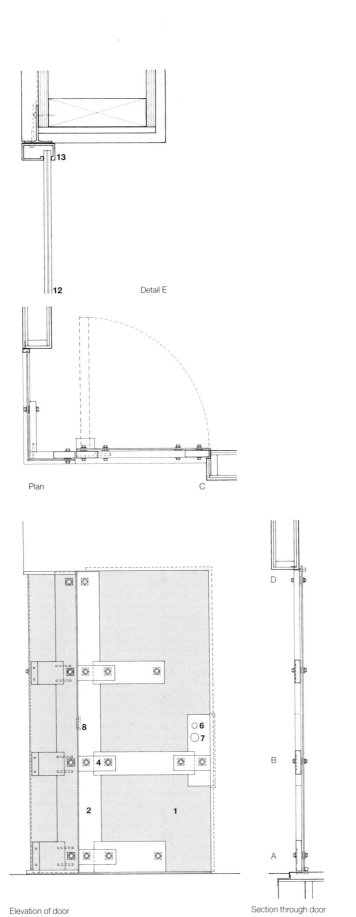

Section through window   Elevation of window   Elevation of door   Section through door

0   50mm

0   2ins

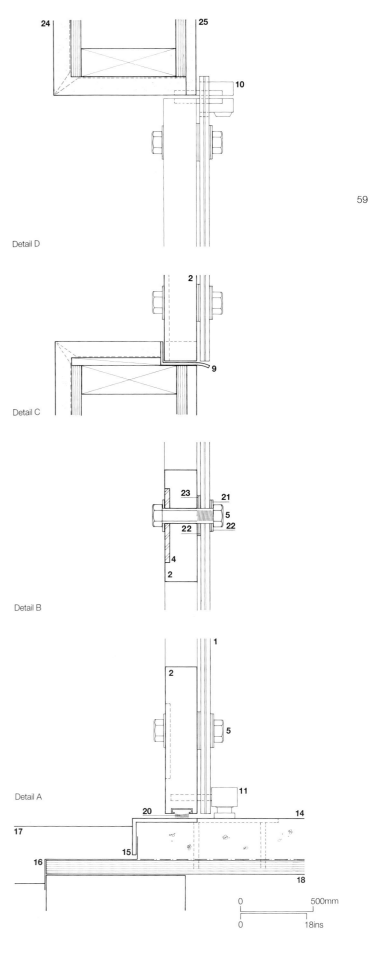

Detail D

Detail C

Detail B

Detail A

0   500mm

0   18ins

Author's acknowledgements

60

I would like to thank Eric Owen Moss, Maureen Moss and Tamara Gould of Eric Owen Moss Architects; Linda Lawson and Tracy Westen for their cooperation in providing information to me; and Julia Doran. I would also like to acknowledge the assistance of Joanna Newson in helping me realize the work, and Victor Regnier for his support.

Illustration acknowledgements

The following illustrations were provided courtesy of: Todd Conversano: figs 11–14, 22, 24, 25, 34–36, 37, 39, 60, 61, 63, 68; LA Aerial Photography: figs 8, 9; Tim Street-Porter: figs 1–3, 56.

Notes

1 See Denise Scott Brown, 'On Houses and Housing', in *Venturi and Scott Brown Monograph No 21* (London: Academy, 1991), p 11. She writes: 'There was a time, not long ago, when many architects, perhaps most young architects, wanted to be housers. Architects of the Modern Movement saw social housing and architecture as virtually coterminous. Their plans for a brave new world figured mainly housing … Architects whose biggest commission was a small house dreamed of cities for millions, the individual house was deemed an unworthy design task, unless it was treated as a point of departure of prototype for mass housing.'

2 Client letter to Eric Owen Moss dated 11 November 1988, p 3.

3 *Ibid*, p 3.

4 'Lawson-Westen House', *Progressive Architecture*, May 1993, p 73.

5 Client letter, 6 December 1988, p 1.

6 *Eric Owen Moss*, Architectural Monograph No 29, James Steele (ed) (London: Academy, 1993), pp 120–1.

7 John Wilton-Ely, *Piranesi*, (London: Arts Council, 1978), p 72.

8 *Ibid*, p 73.

9 Peter Eisenman, 'Visions Unfolding: Architecture in the Age of Electronic Media', *Domus* 22, No 734, January 1992, p 22.

10 *Ibid*, p 23.

11 Rudolf Wittkower, *Architectural Principles in the Age of Humanism* (London: Academy, 1988), p 152.

12 *Ibid*, p 153.

13 Robert Venturi and Denise Scott Brown, lecture entitled 'Architecture as Elemental Shelter, the City as Valid Deacon', delivered in London, 29 April 1991.

14 Witold Rybczynski, *Home: A Short History of an Idea*, (London: Penguin, 1986), p 25.

15 *Ibid*, p 32.

16 Fritz Neumeyer, 'Beyond Narratives: The Architectural Object as Representation of a Methodology of Making and Communication', *A+U*, November 1989, p 37.

17 Lindsay Waters, *Paul de Man: Critical Writings, 1953–1978* (Minneapolis: University of Minnesota Press, 1988), p III.

18 *Ibid*, p IV.

19 Jacques Derrida, 'Memories of Paul de Man', Welleck Library Lecture, translated by Cecile Lindsay, Jonathan Cullen, Eduardo Cudava, Irvine, CA, 1989, p 7.

20 *Progressive Architecture*, *op cit*.

Select bibliography

Eric Owen Moss – Buildings and Projects (New York: Rizzoli, 1995)

Eric Owen Moss (Architectural Monograph No 29) (London: Academy Editions, 1993)

Contemporary American Architects, ed P Jojido (Cologne: Taschen, 1993)

(articles)
'Profile of Eric Owen Moss' by Joseph Giovannini, *Harper's Bazaar,* September 1992
'Lawson-Westen House', *GA Houses* 38, July 1993
'Lawson-Westen House', *A+U*, September 1993
'Forum' section (letter from Eric Owen Moss to *LA Architect* and letter from Linda Lawson, 'A Happy Client'), *LA Architect*, October/November 1993
'Lawson-Westen House', by Michael Webb, *House and Garden*, April 1994
'Lawson-Westen House', *L'Architecture d'Aujourd'hui*, 15 April 1994
'Lawson-Westen House' by Susan Zevon, *House Beautiful*, September 1994

Statistics

Clients
Linda Lawson and Tracy Westen
Architect
Eric Owen Moss
Project associate
Jay Vanos
Project team
Todd Conversano
Jae Lim
Jennifer Rakow
Sheng-yuan Hwang
Scott M Nakao
Dana Swinsky Cantelmo
Amanda Hyde
Elissa Scrafano
Augis Gedgaudas
Mark Lehman
Eric Holmquist
Sophie Harvey
Christine Lawson
Andreas Aug
Urs Padrun
Christoph Lueder
Structural engineer
Gary Davis,
Davis Design Group/
Davis-Fejes Design
Mechanical engineer
Greg Tchamitchian,
AEC Systems
Lighting consultant
Saul Goldin,
Saul Goldin and Associates
Landscape design
Rolla J Wilhite, ASLA with
Linda Lawson
Kitchen design consultant
David Weiss,
Weiss Kitchens
Furniture/fixture fabrication
Tom Farrage,
Farrage & Co
General contractor
John Blackley,
Admiral Construction

Interior/exterior paint
Courtesy of Dunn Edwards Paint
& Wallcoverings
Ceramic tile
Courtesy of Dal-Tile
Kitchen sinks and faucets, below-counter refrigerator, bathroom lavatories
Courtesy of Elkay
Manufacturing Corp
Bathroom faucets
Courtesy of Dornbracht
Bathroom tubs and water closets
Courtesy of Kohler
Interior Design Consultant
Tracy Sonka Stultz, ASID
HTS Architectural Interiors

Chronology

November 1988
Preliminary design begins

February 1989
Preliminary programme completed

June 1989
Schematic design completed

June 1990
Construction documents completed

September 1990
Construction begins

March 1993
Construction completed